Free video training – *How-to theme early childhood art with story books. Sign-up @ www.Montessori-Art.com*

Nature of Art For Kids® Publishing
P.O. Box 443, Solana Beach, California 92075
http://nature-of-art-kids.com

This book may be purchased for educational sales promotional use.

First Edition

Author Spramani Elaun

Designed by Spramani Elaun

Subject: Children's Art/Art Education

Library of Congress Cataloging-in-Publication Data is available upon request.

Contributing Editors: Djani Schafer

All artwork and photographs were taken in an art classroom or at special art events hosted By Spramani Elaun.
© 2019 All rights reserved.

Contributing Photographers: Spramani Elaun, Mandy Sicard, Mike Hedge, Shirley Hadley, Jordann Tomasek, Laurun Cruz

For my international friends, who remind me all children
around the world need art in their life.

Table of Contents

The Importance of Early Art Literacy

Art literacy provides a structure for students to work through the artistic process throughout their education, following national and international visual art standards. To ensure true art literacy, children must directly engage in four actions while creating art: investigate, imagine, construct, and reflect. It is important to teach children visual arts because:

The arts are a unique form of human communication.

The arts foster skills of critical creative thinking and problem solving.

The arts are tools for multicultural understanding.

The arts are a way to understand the social, historical, and cultural contexts

of work from students' own countries.

The arts cultivate pleasure and enjoyment and foster a sense of wellbeing.

Art making stimulates brain development.

Visual arts helps children enter creative flow states.

Art Making in Early Childhood Can Build Brain Intelligence

Motion and Movement Benefits

You may think art-making activities are for filling in gaps of time or just busy work for early childhood students. However, the truth is that the physical movement of art creation results in positive outcomes for children's brain development. When you implement daily movement activities into the curriculum, you're helping students build their hand-eye muscle coordination. I'm talking about the small muscles around the eyes and hands. Most art creation uses hand dexterity and sensorimotor learning for developing muscle memory. This supports gross motor movement into fine motor development. Educators can play a vital role in designing movement activities and what they offer their classrooms.

In recent years, science researchers have established that early motor movement develops better cognitive and academic performance in the later grades (Jan Piek, Lisa Dawson, Leigh Smith, Natalie Gasson, February 2008, "The Role of Early Fine and Gross Motor Development on Later Motor and Cognitive Ability" School of Psychology, Curtin University of Technology Children). Students that practice motor movement early, even starting in infancy, can directly affect cognitive development and their readiness for learning. Researchers explain how children's genetic profiles and experiences can predict good future cognitive performance. Studies done in the United Kingdom have also found correlations with typical motor milestones and their direct effects on cognitive development when children begin primary school. Lack of opportunities to use gross and fine motor movement leaves young students at risk in their physical readiness for being independent when reaching primary grades. Aside from other important aspects of development, such as nutrition, emotional stability, and social support, gross-to-fine-motor movements have been linked to stimulating higher cognitive processes.

Movements provide vital information for the developing nervous system, since it is connected to our multisensory systems wiring for tactile, audio, visual, and balance. Movement also gives the brain stimulating feedback received from motion and movements. This feedback stimulates more sensory inputs, opposed to just looking at something. When movement is involved, neural networks are better stimulated. The experience of movement is a constant neural-looping feedback helping cognition. In other words, it's better for kids to learn when they are moving as opposed to just reviewing audio sound and visual sensory input alone.

This ability helps with complex hand dexterity, intake integration of multi-sensory stimuli, and adjusting motor control, thus developing both neurological and sensorimotor control. In fact, students can benefit tremendously by starting art programs in their early childhood. Art making helps wire cognitive networks to support balance and muscle tone at a young age. Early childhood children eventually need to develop fine-motor skills to use tools like pencils to do their academic task. Additionally, hand dexterity and sensorimotor development is needed to study other domains of visual arts. Over years of practicing these movements, students can increase virtuosity in their hand movements. So, visual arts are fantastic for the brain, and art making in early childhood can build brain intelligence.

John Rubenstein, Pasko Rakic, "Neural Circuit and Cognitive Development:, 2020, 2nd ed

Gross To Fine-Motor Skills

Visual arts provides children with the opportunity to use their hands on a regular basis—holding pencils, pinching and sculpting clay, cutting with scissors, and making fluid brushstrokes all help kids build their hand muscles and strengthen their hand-eye coordination as well as fine motor movements.

Connection to Vocabulary and Communication

Visual arts help kids make connections across different subjects and ideas to be able to better understand things. So when kids explore different art activities, they're actually learning how to communicate what they see in their artworks and how to describe the artistic process they used to create. In doing this, they unknowingly start making observations such as, "I see color," "I see pink," "I see a squiggly line," "I see zigzags." When they communicate those observations to you or each other, they begin to develop their art language and a greater vocabulary, which is important cognitive processing.

Stress Regulation

Creating art also helps children wire their brains to regulate stress. Art gives them the tools to learn how to calm themselves down. Tactile sensory processing occurs when children create art; neural networks fire and signal their focus solely on what they're doing with their hands, blocking outside thoughts and stimuli. What happens is, if kids are stressed out or upset about something and they're making art, they can't focus on that. Art involves active learning, meaning they have to focus on what they're doing immediately, which takes away the upsetting, stressful things that are happening in their environment.

Implicit Memory

Another area of brain development art fuels is implicit memory. When kids learn repeated movements, they're strengthening their implicit memory and are actually storing this new information. The next time that they engage in an art activity, implicit memory kicks in and their hand movements will come naturally—the actions are wired and become linked in their brain. That means they don't have to consciously think about every minute action; they will see a paintbrush, and instinctively know to pick it up, dip it into the palette or water, and start creating. The sensory information of seeing the paintbrush and then holding it in their hand immediately sends that information to their brain, triggering an action. Building this implicit memory helps develop more skills down the road; they'll have this implicit memory already stored in their brain and can then focus new skills to learn.

Spatial Intelligence

Spatial intelligence is learned through creating with forms in space. When children make art, they become aware of the spatial relationships among objects in the realm of their own experiences. This gives them the ability to visualize and manipulate elements, rotate objects, and distinguish depth and balance—which is critical in early childhood brain development. It's important to note that spatial intelligence is something that cannot be taught unless kids are actually doing an activity; art gives them the experience

The Artist Language We Teach

Art does have its own language, it's called the 'Elements and Principles of Design' but that's way too advanced for early childhood students to understand. When you talk to young children about art—"Artist Language"—it's really just describing what you see in artworks, like color, shape, line, etc.

The Elements and Principles of Design teaches children how to communicate what they see in their artworks, as well as how to describe their process and explain what they admire in artworks. You don't have to use "art language," proper terminology, or fancy words in order for them to start appreciating, introducing, or experiencing art. If you were to jump right in with this kind of terminology, you're going to lose the child's attention, confuse them, and likely get frustrated yourself. When you're first introducing art language keep things basic and simple.

Start by describing what you see when you're looking at art or what's going on as you make art. As they explore more and more and start really getting to know what art is, using art language will become easier. More than likely, their inquisitive little minds will start making connections (like, "if I use this color paint and this paintbrush, it'll come out like this"), and they'll probably start asking questions (such as, "what color is this?" or "why did this do this?").

Elements and Principles of Design is also known as the Elements of Art:

Line

Color

Shape

Form

Space

Texture & Pattern

Value

Symmetry

2 Dimensions

3 Dimensions

Composition

Here are some examples of how to use art language with young kids. While reading story books point out colors, try,

"The fox is all green, would you like to color something green today like this fox?"

"Let's cut out some shapes, like circles and squares, with scissors."

"Hey, what about making some textures in our clay!"
(You can use stamps, textured or embossed rolling pins, or even pressing dried beans into clay to create texture.)

"Let's make some squiggly lines and straight lines. How many different colored lines can we do?"

"Let me show you how to make a brand new color by mixing these two primary colors. Look how the yellow and blue mix, what color does it make?"
(Recommended for ages 4-6.)

Which Elements Do You Teach First?

Teaching children art language starts with understanding the differences in the elements. Naturally, we need to introduce students to these art words. Our role as the facilitator is to build this rich visual arts vocabulary. Helping children build this vocabulary allows them to tell us what they see in artworks or even helps them describe their own process. So, in what order should you start introducing the elements and principles of design to early childhood education? I recommend starting with the easiest, then build up to the more complex elements.

There is no right or wrong way to teach the elements; this is my own system for teaching visual arts. I've found this order helps children understand my art instruction much better and is less confusing. I start with basic concrete ideas children can relate to in their everyday lives and schoolwork. Then, I move into more abstract principles, which helps build onto more complex skillsets. So, first start with easy elements children can understand before moving to more abstract elements and principles. Over time, I've noticed that teaching in this order helps children learn to draw and paint faster in the elementary grades. You will find some children in the later phase of early childhood (around 4, 5, and 6 years old) are able to recognize these elements quickly and ready to learn.

I start this order with (1) LINE, (2) SHAPE, (3) COLOR, and (4) FORM. Once children have a good understanding of these four elements, I'll introduce the fifth element, TEXTURE and PATTERN. Then, when my students' attention span is longer and they can concentrate more and plan with intention, I introduce the sixth element, SPACE, followed by the seventh element, VALUE, and eighth element, SYMMETRY. Finally, I end with COMPOSITION. Children should first understand these elements and principles before advancing to any other art principles.

Young children start out by scribbling in a circular motion. So, I start with lines, shapes, and colors. Once they get full control of their marks, they can transition into creating closed shapes. Then, they can learn to color these shapes solid. Once that is learned, children can move to making texture and pattern marks over their shapes. Afterward, you can teach children color theory concepts like warm, cool, primary, secondary, and complimentary colors. Then, children can focus on space and symmetry. When children begin wanting to make their drawings and paintings more real-looking, you can introduce value and composition concepts. So, this is my reason for teaching the elements in this order. This is how I start teaching children to draw and paint by understanding the basic elements and principles of design.

Early childhood art lessons should only isolate one element per lesson. Can you teach more than one element at a time? Yes. But don't confuse children. Be sure they have a clear understanding of one element first before you combine it with a new element. It's just like blending the alphabet sounds. You must first teach the sound of one alphabet before you can have them blend two letters together. Eventually, they can sound the

whole word. This is also similar to Parts to Whole teaching. You can combine line and shape, shape and color, line and color, form and texture, color and value, and shape and space.

Each lesson should build one skill at a time. Give young children plenty of time to revisit these lessons and practice. Remember, we are introducing art language, and we should not expect children to copy these elements exactly. Introduce them, model these movements, and give good visual inspiration examples to look at. If a child is capable and interested, great! But do not require children to copy exactly what you put forward. Try to remember that children at these ages need process-based experiences to explore and discover these new ideas. You might have to stage and demonstrate five different art activities, focusing on just one element for all your students to fully understand and make the connection to the visual idea and the art language. The truth is, we are trying to build their long-term memory. So, take it slow and have fun.

What You Should Teach, and the Order:

Lines - Wiggly, curve, wavey, straight horizontal and vertical lines, zig zag, diagonal, swirls, dots, dashes, thick, and thin lines.

Shape - Start with organic shapes like fruit, leaves, flowers, animals, eggs, shapes in nature, moon, clouds, the sun, stars, and hearts. Next, teach geometric shapes like the circle, square, triangle, rectangle, and hexagon.

Color - Start with primary colors (red, yellow, and blue), secondary colors (orange, green, and violet), spectrum of colors (rainbow), warm colors, cool colors, black, and grey.

Forms - Teach form with clay modeling in solid forms, such as sphere, egg, cube, cone, cylinder, flat pancake, snake (coil), and pyramid before teaching organic forms.

Texture & Pattern - Lines in different directions, patterns in dotted lines and solids, organic shape patterns in lines or solids, geometric shapes in patterns in lines and textures, hair lines, grass, fish scales, wood grain, lines in leaves, water waves, lines in bird feathers, lines in plants, rain drops, spider webs, spotted animals, lines in seashells, lines in bumpy texture, soft texture, and prickly texture. Patterns and textures are endless, but they start with lines and shapes.

Space - Show children how space is interchangeable in both how their elements are spaced apart from each other or arranged in a space. You can point out space in their composition and how the space is balanced, positive, or negative.

Value - Teach children color value with dry and wet mediums. Show them how to mix their own values with wet liquid paints by creating light color values, medium values, and dark values. You can also show them how to create values with dry drawing mediums to get each color to a light, medium, and dark value by applying pressure to each color.

Symmetry - Teach kids very basic line symmetry. Show children how each shape has an exact resemblance to its other part.

The Art Subjects We Teach

5 Domains

Children in early childhood should have a foundation in five specific areas if they're going to learn art. I call these areas The 5 Domains. If they can learn these areas, they will have a good foundation for mastering further advanced concepts needed in the upper grades.

The 5 Domains:

Drawing
Painting
Color Theory (Color Wheel Mixing)
Clay Modeling
Crafting

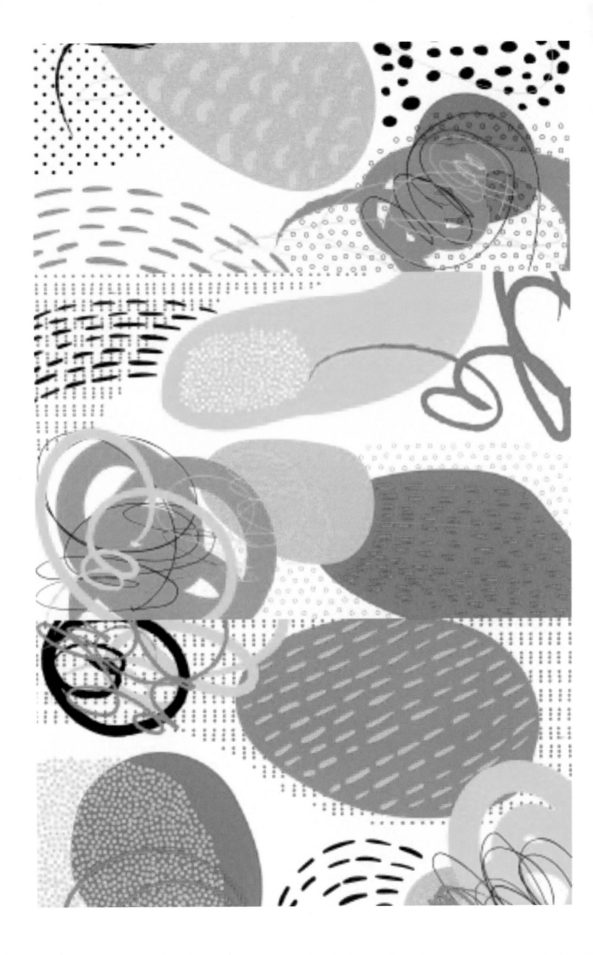

Drawing

Doodling Comes First

Doodling is the first stage to learning to draw. Drawing is the most common way children create line form. You will find that, as children gain finemotor skills, drawing and doodling become daily activities. A child's first marks are in line and there are many reasons for this. Simple line marks are easier for a child to see and comprehend because there are no difficult rendering details, just dark lines. Dark lines against light colored paper are much easier for their retinas to detect. Doodling is simple free style drawing by making lines without three dimensional perspectives. It occurs at the same time children learn to write.

Doodling can be driven by many playful imaginative ideas. Doodling can also be a way for a child to express their emotions. Many opportunities for doodling freely should be allowed in early childhood. You should not correct a child's doodles. It's very healthy for a child to be doodling and draw this way.

Students Aged 3-6 Are Not Ready for Formal Drawing Lessons

Writing and holding a pencil is not readiness for teaching a young child drawing lessons. There are many reasons why adults or teachers may think this is true. First young children are capable of duplicating 26 letters of the alphabet and ten numbers. Writing comes naturally for a child, because letters are solid light information for visual pathways to sense. Letters and numbers are similar because they use straight and simple curved lines. Learning the alphabet uses other sensory inputs like touch, vision, and linguistic sound. When all sensory systems are used cognitive processing helps children learn difficult concepts more easily.

In a short time children can achieve dexterity with a pencil. Simple shapes like circles, ovals, and straight lines can be learned quickly. Learning to write can come easily for young children but doesn't necessarily prepare them for advanced drawing lessons. Line forms and symbolic imagery are what needs to be learned first when learning how to draw. Generally drawings are inspired by creative-mode, but in this later phase students can be instructed on simple and easy copy-mode drawing work.

What is Creative-Mode Drawing?

Creative Mode refers to how I nurture child-led art projects. I introduce a project, demonstrate the medium, and usually give no point of reference (an image to copy). The child creates art by exploring the medium and conjuring up creative images from their own imaginations. Creative imagination is thoughts and ideas that emerge from one's own personal reflections.

What is Copy-Mode Drawing?

Copy-mode refers to a systematic, step-by-step art instruction. But in early childhood, you don't want to yet introduce copy-what-you-see type of lessons. At this stage, children love to mimic an easy task they see adults do, such as sweeping, cleaning, sewing, painting, cutting, and gardening. Bring this same idea into your art lessons and allow them to copy your movements and simple organic and geometric line shapes.

Toddler Doodling

Toddlers doodle without any real control, but they do enjoy playing with crayons and color pencils, and they love to start to mimic adults that are making marks. They go through a phase of grasping and holding and then eventually understanding that they're making marks and some drawing control happens around age three.

Ages 3-6 Drawing

Children are now excited to be challenged to make basic shapes in the later phase of these ages, such as images of stick people, animals, and plants. At these ages you can now teach kids how to control doodles and help them understand sketching pressure. Give kids fun, easy lines exercise like point to line, line marks in different directions, curved lines, curvy lines, curvy lines into rounded shapes, and squiggly curved lines to build their fine-motor abilities. You can point these elements out in all the topics your learning like, "Look at the lines on this leaf," or "look how this snake curves into a coil." Other teachable examples may be: follow your finger on this labyrinth's curved path, carve lines into your clay, look at how the snowflake design is made of lines, can you see the wavy water lines in this picture, what line patterns do you see in this animal, etc.

By the later phase of this plane children should be able to make basic controlled geometric common shapes, and simple line organic shapes like a leaf, a tree outline, star, stick humans, line flower shapes. Introduce copy-mode by having students copy simple shapes (one or two steps). Once they have the basic design complete, let them continue on in creative-mode and finish their projects
however they want.

27

Painting

Painting

Similar to doodling, painting can also start out with gross motor abilities then develop to fine-motor with line and texture marks. Painting is achieved by pigments and brushstrokes. Printmaking is also included in the painting domain, but uses different types of tools and materials. You can introduce painting concepts to children as young as 13 months.

Children love to play with paint. At these ages, painting is more of an exploratory experience and not so much about what picture to paint. Young kids should paint in a playful discovery way. Painting lessons should be at the level of the young child's abilities. Kids lack the ability to plan out detailed, realistic paintings in the beginning years.

Kids need plenty of time to learn how paint behaves and what its application possibilities are. Don't expect young kids to start painting realistic paintings or be able to copy pictures of images clearly. Working in copy-mode is very difficult for young kids at these ages.

However, some kids at ages 3-6 can work in copy-mode or mimic images to a degree, in a playful manner and without pressure. Some images are easier for young kids to replicate than others. Lots of painting practice and experience will help a child become a better painter. Children in the later phase of early childhood are open to simple brush stroke lessons.

Toddler Painting

Toddlers start to paint and love to make the movements, however, their painting marks are uncontrollable until they get some grasping practice. They love to enjoy making the actions of painting and mimicking adult paint brush strokes. At this age, they can dip a paintbrush into a palette and load it with paint, make a brush mark onto a surface, and clean their brush using a wash jar. Their painting involves very simple brush stroke marks. Kids also love using their fingers and exploring creating with tools like sponges and rollers. You don't want to do any directed painting lessons with toddlers; rather, lead them through very simple and easy-flow type projects.

Remember toddlers are exploring with their mouths, so they will eat paint. You want to make sure that any paint you use is earth-friendly, safe, and non-toxic for them. You can even make homemade paint with fruit and vegetable dyes. But you definitely want to remember that kids do eat paint—expect it. They usually grow out of that impulse between the ages of two-and-a-half and three years old.

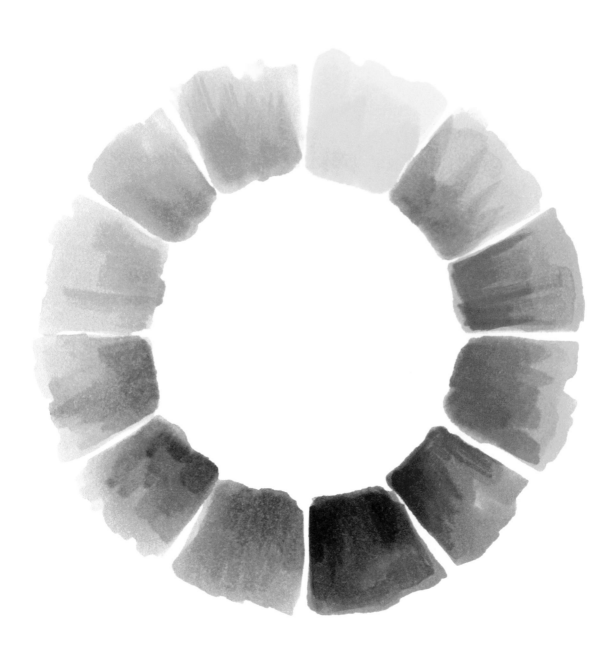

Color Theory

Color Theory

Color theory is a simple way to discover how color behaves and can transform into new colors. Color theory starts with the very basic colors of red, yellow, and blue. Color theory exploration in the younger years builds excellent spatial learning and is very healthy for children to experience. Color theory is even therapeutic. It's a simple, natural way for kids to learn the basis of color; it introduces color to them in a way that meets their level of understanding and comprehension. I recommend lots of process-based color experiences (I explain the idea of process-based activities in another chapter of this book).

Color theory can be combined with painting activities. You will later come to understand the materials for color theory are similar to the painting domain. Make sure lots of color play is included in your programming and that you're offering it throughout the year.
Toddlers can start to recognize colors, and kids ages 3-6 usually know all the colors of the rainbow. Children in the later phase can start simple color theory mixing lessons. I've included a color mixing activities at the end of this book.

Clay Modeling

Clay Modeling

This domain supports hands-on sensory tactile spatial learning by modeling clay. Children love playing with clay. Young children build modeling skills by manipulating clay by hand or with sculpture tools. There are many types of organic and inorganic clay matter that can be used for this domain.

Clay forming helps children understand solid three-dimensional creating in both static and dynamic motion. Children who have opportunities to build, model, and sculpt geometric or organic sculptures gain spatial awareness much better. Many art lessons can be integrated into the curriculum by using clay modeling. I've included some basic lesson ideas at the back of this book. Children aged 3-6 are ready for simple modeling forming lessons.

Crafting

Crafting

Many different materials can be used to craft or build with. The main focus of these projects is usually developing great spatial-cognitive learning. Crafting and constructing usually produces a three-dimensional piece of artwork.

Toddler Crafting

These ages will probably be limited to very basic movements because kids are just learning to hold and grasp things. They can only do very simple type projects. I'd recommend waiting until age three to begin introducing crafting projects. You want to always be available to supervise young children when crafting with little embellishments. Adults can assist by embellishing the students' creations for them, to safely help make connections to inspiration sample ideas, like adding googly eyes to make a creature, or adding feathers.

Ages 3-6 Crafting

Children aged 3-6 can start formal sewing, glueing, cutting, collaging, paper folding, weaving, and woodworking. Children's gross motor abilities are developing into fine-motor skills and they are no longer putting small items into their mouths, this is the best time to start handicrafts.

Child Artist Characteristics

Child Artist Characteristics

A child in early development, when given a paintbrush, paper, and paints, is in a very curious state. Art is very discovery, very exploratory, and very hands-on. At these ages, children cannot follow directions. In this plane, there is no planning with intention. Kids in this phase are not prepared for that kind of preparation. So if you wanted to bring out a project where the child has to follow directions and have a plan, it's not going to work. Art project making should be simple and not complex with step-by-step instructions. You simply want children to experience art making (as a process-based activity).

Inherited and environmental factors can also play a role in each child's skill level; even the opportunities and privilege to be exposed to art lessons make a difference. Kids develop at different rates around the world. Some of these factors are based on nutrition, cultural background, or social activities from country to country. This could explain why some kids are quicker to learn art skills than other kids. I recommend that you don't compare a child's skills over another child's abilities at any age, but especially during early childhood.

A child's artistic development is related to their sensory system, cognitive functioning, gross-to-fine-motor growth, and much more. I'll discuss how to best approach teaching visual arts to early childhood students in the next chapter.

Yes, Early Childhood Children Can Be Taught Real Art Skills!

I've taught thousands of toddlers how to make a brushstroke, dip a paintbrush into a wash jar to clean their brush off, then dip their paintbrush into a palette to change colors for their next mark. And I've also watched their growth and excitement when they finally make an intentional shape. I'm sure you've witnessed the same thing with your students learning to write their first letters, button their shirts, or sound out their first word. Art skills are taught the very same way, meaning you teach a lesson and you're their guide.

You'll read throughout this book how children are not developmentally ready for advanced art steps, or planning with intention, or even seeing with an aesthetic eye. However, what you'll come to understand is that you can plan, and you can set an intention to provide the child the opportunity to learn by example. You can make the necessary preparations, stage the right materials, and have the willingness to give the child the invitation to explore.

Far too many times I meet teachers that set up art supplies and walk away thinking the art supplies will teach skills or entertain their students, not understanding why art making becomes chaotic and messy. When I introduce toddlers to an art lessons I stay right beside them at their eye level through the entirety of the session. I create and demonstrate artistic movements so the child can observe my technique. I make the correct movements so the child can start to understand what the mediums are capable of. My students also get inspired by my creations. When we are done working you will see their artworks right beside my artwork. This is why I've been a very successful art teacher—I allow the student to be the observer.

Methods & Approaches to Teaching

Based on my naturalistic observations working with tens of thousands children of all ages in real studio practice, in all five domains, I've structured this method and its approaches through my experiences getting consistent results in developing skillful artists. The structures in this chapter are my methods to nurturing early childhood visual arts.

All sequences of instructions can be the same but will never affect each individual child in the same way. This means that every child cognitively processes information differently, depending on their developmental stage in life and experience, knowledge, and interests. Young kids in this phase can't look at projects with planning. I recommend not introducing advanced lessons and keeping projects basic. Simple child-led activities are healthy for children at these young ages. Free form making should be introduced, with no complex steps to follow. Plenty of hand manipulations while playing with most mediums listed in this book are great for fine-motor development.

Toddler Concentration Time

As far as concentration level, I schedule 20 minutes to 40 minutes for art activities. You don't want to do anything past 40 minutes. In fact, the very first few times that children encounter visual arts and exploring like this, it's usually a few minutes, and they'll walk away because they don't really understand what's happening.

As toddlers start getting used to touching mediums, understanding what's happening, and seeing things unfold, it sparks their curiosity and they become eager to start exploring. They will also come to know why the materials are out and what to do with them. Once a child understands what is happening in the actions of art-making, they become more interested, and the concentration levels start to last a little bit longer. So start off with a few minutes, expand to 15 minutes, then 20 once children get familiar with art mediums. You will probably find yourself setting up longer than it takes for them to actually explore art, but don't get discouraged. Once you get in the system of setting up projects for your kids and you start bringing these art projects into your early childhood classroom, your students will get used to it and get accustomed to it, and they'll start to enjoy and explore and you'll start to see some art-making happen. So don't worry, it gets better.

Ages 3–6 Concentration Time

Children aged 3-4 can work up to 20 to 40 minutes, and children 5–-6 can work from 40 to 60 minutes. Gross motor abilities are now fine and controlled, and they have the attention span to listen to simple guided 1- to 2-step instructions. These children now have vivid and creative imaginations and like to work independently.

Learning Through Process-Based Art

The best instruction method to introducing art lessons is through process-based art making. Process-based art is about the experience and the process; it's not focused on the child's final piece of artwork or whether it resembles art adults can recognize, but rather, it's about exploring and using their own imagination. With process based art, you're not worrying about what a finished artwork is going to look like. Also, with process-based art, time is irrelevant, meaning students can go back and add to an older project during a different art-making session.

Young students are not yet ready to make realistic pictures or aesthetically pleasing finished artworks; they'll be able to learn more advanced skills later in life. At this age, they're simply at a stage of exploration. Their learning and development of problem-solving skills come from spending time making process-based art. When kids get to freely play and express themselves, they're gaining the ability to think creatively. Discovery and experimentation are key to process-based art making.

Give students opportunities to focus on experimentation. However, you should present a light, very simplistic introductory demonstrations on how mediums can work or be used. I recommend showing how mediums might turn out and the different techniques that can be achieved with each. This empowers children with the confidence to create. Make sure they know that any type of exploration is good, and there is no wrong way to use mediums and attempt whatever they choose to create.

Most Common Process-Based Art Mistakes

As well-intentioned as teachers may be when it comes to art instruction, if teaching process-based art is new to them, they're prone to making a few mistakes.

Here are five dos and don'ts for giving your students process art experiences.

1. Don't introduce art lessons as step-by-step instructions (this is known as copy mode, and can be shared with students at an older age). Instead, do give children the freedom to create outside of specific instruction.

2. Don't tell children that their project has a right way and wrong way to be created. Do encourage them to explore and assure them that anything they make is accepted.

3. Don't expect a child's finished art to look the same as a sample, or even be a recognizable image. Do remember that in early childhood, students are still grasping artistic mediums and techniques; what they create will be completely unique to their imagination and abilities.

4. Don't discourage a student from exploring mediums in ways you haven't introduced. Do give them space to experiment and be unique.

5. Don't feel compelled to correct a child or guide them to fix their project to look more like the example. Do remember that process art is about the process, not the finished product.

Imitating Adult Movements is Positive

Children love imitating adults, and can learn by mimicking your movements. This can help them understand what to do with art materials and learn new concepts. I don't want you to misunderstand my idea of imitation as copying exactly what I do. By imitating your movements children can still work in a process-based method. Young kids, of course, will not be able to completely imitate other artworks, but they can inspire ideas. This is positive fine art observation for the young artist. Authentic, creative art making will follow when children learn by imitation at their own pace and without judgement.

Control & Error

It's essential that teachers don't correct or critique children at these ages. Students naturally learn and progress from their mistakes and by observing other students' artist techniques. Observing and waiting for the next lesson is the best opportunity for you to review procedures again. You should never stop a child from working to correct movements. If you like, work next to your students so they can observe your technique. Mistakes are part of the artistic process and development of an artist.

Dismantling Artworks is Normal in Early Childhood

It's quite common for a child to create a beautiful decorated form and later dismantle it or pick it apart afterwards. Believe it or not, dismantling and destroying art is a learning process children need to experience. It's normal for children between the ages of 2-6 years to dismantle out of curiosity. These experiences help children have deep levels of thoughts and understand ideas. Creating in this style can build strong foundations of understanding their physical world. Dismantling can be just as important as the action of assembling forms. Children at these young ages are not overly concerned with producing an end product for display, but more so on the curious physical process and sensory stimulation they're learning from. Older children have the abilities to create forms with an intention or plan and are less likely to dismantle their creations.

Tip: If your student creates a project you want to save as a keepsake, I recommend you quickly move it out of the reach of your busy little artist or dismantler.

Share Positive Inspirational Artworks

Some fine artists' works are good to have hanging in your classroom's art space, but should not be the only examples kids see. I understand that this is how most Montessori schools engage students in observing fine arts. However, I've spent many years concentrating on understanding how a child's visual perception develops and I've found that advanced fine art skill building does not work—in fact, it can even stifle creativity early on.

 I don't recommend heavily decorating the classroom with advanced fine artworks or working solely with these types of pictures, cards, or curriculum during early childhood. Lots of hands-on art making needs to happen before young children can look at fine art prints and relate to or observe their techniques. They're even too young to appreciate it. Instead, display artworks from their peers or other children; they'll be able to observe work that's closer to their level, notice techniques, and with excitement, want to try it out for themselves.

It's also important to point out that viewing fine artist works in 2-dimension alone offers reduced field of vision to learn from; children learn and comprehend much better by their own sensory inputs. Real spatial art making must be the child's primary way of developing fine art skills, not simply studying advanced fine artist paintings and techniques through observation alone. This kind of studying comes much later, in the adolescent years.

Staging Nature-Based Inspiration

Lots of hands-on art making at the child's level of understanding is where most inner creativity is sparked. You can stage and load art shelves with nature-based ideas to be wonderful springboard for inspiration. This supports art making that's understood by their evolving visual perception and ongoing topic-work in the classroom (Child to World).

I always display nature-based collections that children understand, can relate to, and are learning about. I use pictures, posters, books, and real collections of objects arranged around my art shelves.

Things such as leaves, feathers, weeds, seeds, beans, rocks, seashells, seasonal fruits, and flowers. I also hang pictures or posters of insects, butterflies, birds, or sea life—all at eye level. You change these out seasonally to reflect your current studies. Staging shelves with nature-based inspiration can be very simple to more complex, but it will always be a great source for creative art making ideas. A gallery of art inspiration is very helpful in the Montessori classroom and promotes creative thinking and idea development.

Supportive Words Help Self-esteem in Creating

When kids share their artworks, it's important to remember they are in the beginning phases of their lives and creating visual arts. It can take many hours of practicing to paint pictures that are recognizable to adults. My advice is to listen first, and try NOT to be quick to ask questions about what they painted or why. Help children feel confident by listening. Listening can help them talk about what's on their mind or describe their artworks. Listening is very supportive and won't make a child feel judged or bring focus to their artistic skills.

One of the most common mistakes teachers and parents make is asking children too many questions about what they created or trying to analyze it like an art critic. Sometimes children will agree with your questions or comments to please you. Kids under the age of six years old are not yet aware of adult artistic terms (or artist language) like lines, form, sketching, composition, space, or color theory. Some new students may have not yet had enough art language exposure to understand these terms in context.

Art Making: Sensory & Tactile

Tactile learning can be described as learning through touching with one's own hands. When a child touches an object, messages of information are sent through sensory nerves to the brain. Tactile sensory experiences can help young children learn and understand ideas. Visual art learning can happen from direct sensory touching by hands. Tactile art making stimulates learning in different ways than visual or audio learning. For a developing child, tactile exploring can also lead to better fine-motor function and control. Tactile learning is recommended for highly active children or kinesthetic learning styles. These types of children learn better by physical action and tactile sensations. Visually, hearing, and linguistically impaired children greatly benefit by tactile learning sensations. A child's manipulations or artwork are their understanding from tactile experiences.

It's becoming increasingly important for young children to have sensory tactile exploring opportunities. Doing visual art projects is a perfect way tactile sensation can take place. Almost all art making requires using direct touch to construct, build, or express. Without tactile opportunities, a   child can miss out on important spatial learning. Learning and creating through touch helps with brain connectivity that can't come from just sight and hearing sensory systems.

Sensory tactile art exploration is very important for young children to have. I recommend providing lots of tactile art experiences. Try out many different sensory art projects that can aid in learning and be experienced by hand manipulations. Provide lots of blocks of time for using hands and fingers directly.

Tactile Art Making Is Beneficial for Stress Relief

I've witnessed tactile art projects lead to relaxation. Most art activities are multi-sensory engaging and can help kids relax and play calmly. Tactile touching induces stimulating neural input from most senses. When a young child starts drawing, painting, touching, and forming, it's considered active learning. Hand art making stimulates touch input; a child's visual pathways communicate with both left and right hemispheres of the brain, and auditory and smell sensory systems are also collecting information. Art making is high in visual-auditory connectivity in the brain. Strong connectivity occurs and the child becomes intensely focused on his or her handiwork. Children using their hands can be so engaged that other stress-related thoughts clear their minds. The electrical activity stimulated in the brain becomes a different type of action, firing connections that allow children to focus only on their creating process. A calming effect takes place because tactile cognitive processing is occurring while children form and manipulate with their hands. It's good for children during their sensitive periods to develop good habits and activities that can help regulate relaxation by creative handiwork early in life. Tactile art making can relieve stress for kids!

Art Develops Spatial Intelligence; Understanding Space

Spatial learning develops from understanding the relations between objects. Spatial learning is formed after a child gathers tactile sensory information through two types of spatial learning—either through dynamic motion or by viewing static imagery results. This understanding is of perspective space between elements in two dimensions, or geographical placement, or the position of arranging items in three dimensional space. Spatial learning is recorded in our memory, either in the hippocampus or medial temporal lobes of our brain. Visual arts is all about spatial understanding. This is one of the core teachings of the Elements and Principles of Design.

Making art is a significant way to improve visual spatial intelligence. Kids gain spatial intelligence from creating forms in space. They become aware of spatial relations among objects in the realm of their own experiences, giving them the ability to mentally visualize, manipulate elements, rotate objects, design form, and create volume, distinguish depth with value, balance, and understand putting together and building structures.

A child must independently use their own sensory system to acquire spatial perception in either 2-D or 3-D projects. Spatial art intelligence can only take place when the child is the sole or collaborating physical creator. A child cannot gain spatial art intelligence through viewing other artworks without engaging their own sensory systems in the process of creating. Creating in both two and three dimensions supports good spatial awareness. Lots of spatial art making experiences will benefit the child cognitively. Visual art learning also happens after the child is done making art, so be sure to have their artwork displayed where they can see so they can cognitively process the results from their dynamic actions.

Art Develops Fine-Motor Skills

I've spent years observing how young students learn art, and how sensory art-making actions can help students achieve better control of their fine motor skills. Fine motor development is a physical attribute that advances as children grow. Fine motor control helps with creating art projects and using art materials. When fine motor control is achieved, a child can use a paintbrush to make marks, doodle, draw and sketch with a pencil, and sculpt or build with their own hands. Getting fine-tuned motor control takes years for young children, unlike adults. A child gains motor development skills as he learns to control small muscles. These small muscles can be in their fingers, hands, arms, and even the muscles around the eyes. Once a child achieves control of these small muscles, it becomes easier to learn art skills and explore techniques. Gaining mastery in their movements can help children with paintbrush dipping, paintbrush strokes, mixing and achieving colors, grasping, applying and adjusting presure, holding a pencil, making marks or doodling, squeezing, pressing, pushing, manipulating clay into a form, and tearing and cutting hand movements. These movements become possible with full control of muscles. Just like other large muscles, the more you use them, the better control you have over them. Understand that to become artistically skillful, fine motor-control has to happen first.

Provide lots of repetitious art experiences to help children get fine motor control as they grow. Remember, children at the same age can possibly be at different logical and physical phases of development, so lots of repetition is recommended in these early years. All sequences of instruction can be the same, but will never affect each individual child in the same way. This means that every child cognitively processes information differently depending on their developmental stage in life, art experience, knowledge, and interests. Provide multiple art lessons for practice in using large muscles and small muscles. Many art projects can look different but have the same beneficial skill-builing repetition needed for artistic fine-motor control. For example, let children play with large paintbrushes for larger brush strokes, then move to smaller paint brushes for smaller controlled brush strokes with many different projects or the same style of project. Typically, I start my students out with clay modeling, paint brush stroking, and safety scissor activities which all help develop fine motor strength quickly.

Always Demonstrate Technique

Kids Aged 3–6 Years

An artist technique means a way of doing something, or a special way an artist performs basic movements unique to their own style. For these ages all activities should be presented with a technique demonstration, not to instruct students to follow systematic step-by-step instructions or be a copycat, but to inspire the child that's ready and capable of learning a new technique. Remember children develop at different rates physically and cognitively. Giving a demonstration along with an artist example is still a good idea, I call this an inspiration gallery prompt. Children need artistic examples and inspiration to stimulate creative new ideas. You just need to remember that children should not be required to copy, just invited to try it out.

Another reason it's a good idea to introduce a technique from time to time is children may not understand that a medium can function in multiple different ways, producing different results. Let's take for example paper and crayons. The average student may only think he can doodle with a crayon. But, it's much more exciting when you can direct the kids and say, "Now I want to show you a special technique that an artist does with crayons and paper, called wax resist." Then you can show samples and say, "These samples are created by an artist who uses a wax resist technique with crayons." Then suddenly, the kids get ignited to experiment and create with guided direction.

I've observed this time and time again, when kids visit my art studio. Children run into my studio and are excited by all the art supplies available to them, but they don't have enough confidence to create stuff, or they have never been taught any art creating techniques. Once I teach them a technique, oh my gosh, you should see how their confidence and excitement grows and things change. I want you to think about highlighting an artist technique when you decide to introduce an art project to older kids in this plane. They will be much more successful when they are shown different techniques that can be done with art mediums and materials.

Practical Life Activities Don't Replace Art Learning

I want to mention here that Montessori practical life lessons are not designed for children to follow the artistic process. Most practical life activities have step-by-step instructions and procedures. If you would like further learn more about this I offer professional development courses on these topics.

Whole to Parts

Whole to parts can be compared to one domain of study, such as painting. Learning to paint can be broken down into easy, natural lesson parts, which stimulate the child's curiosity. Examples of learning parts of painting could be how to hold a paintbrush, how to clean a paintbrush, how to operate a loaded paint palette, how to make a wide brush stroke, etc.

Child to World

Child to world learning concepts can also relate to how a child develops artistically. Visual art learning is much easier to understand when it's relevant to the child's reality or understanding, rather than starting off with hard to understand abstract ideas like studying a master painter and their techniques. If a young child is learning letters and sounds have them paint alphabet letters; if they're learning about zoology, invite them to create images related to that particular study topic. After some time, children will better relate to the process of art making. As children pass through each art phase you bring them closer to abstract ideas or explaining the Elements and Principles of Design with their concrete artworks.

Conclusion:

If every art activity you provide is supported with process-based concepts, and you move your students through the four artistic actions, you are meeting art literacy standards.

Artistic Process

The Artistic Process is four actions: investigation, imagination, construction, and reflection.

Investigation – Students should have the opportunity to investigate different art projects and a variety of mediums and techniques, through exploration, examination, and discovery.

Imagination – Students should have the opportunity to imagine an original mental image or concept.

Construction – Students should have the opportunity to construct an art project through mediums or arranging art elements.

Reflection – Students should have the opportunity to reflect and think deeply about their arts.

Art Space Environments

Art Space Environments

Early childhood students are curious explorers with short attention spans. It's important to keep this in mind when setting up their art environment. If you're intentional about what you include and how you organize their art-making space, it can have an immensely positive impact on how they learn and appreciate art. A toddler's art environment should be set up purposefully; it's going to look different and have a different function than an art space set up for children 3-6 years old.

Students aged 3-6 years can sit at a table for 30 minutes and follow the simple instructions, while a toddler may only stick around for 5-15 minutes. At either age, art should be hands-on, which means it can get messy—especially with toddlers. The goal is to set up an area designed for exploring and for keeping little ones engaged, as well as containing messes. Most traditional mediums (like paint) can leave pigmented marks that stain clothes and fabrics, so you want to set up an art-making environment that allows for some splashing, splattering, smearing, and dripping. If you do this correctly, you won't need constant supervision and you won't have to worry about excessive clean up.

A Space for Developing Fine-Motor Skills

When thinking about setting up the art environment, it's important to remember that art making in early childhood is an excellent opportunity for them to develop their fine-motor skills. The general idea is to create a safe space so kids can practice their fine motor movements, such as gliding their hands in fingerpaint, making wide brushstrokes, rolling paint rollers, and squeezing, rolling out, and pounding clay. Early childhood students' first interaction with art making is process-based, discovery-based, exploratory, and playful. It's not until they get a little older that they will be able to sit and create with intention. So you want to focus on creating spaces for children to be able to do fine-motor-movement exploring tasks. You want to think about this early phase as learning art mediums through tactile senses, body movements, and seeing and feeling the textures the different mediums create and leave behind.

Art Environment Features

There are several features to consider when setting up a Montessori art space. Here are the elements to include in your child's art space, and the practical reasons I recommend them as an art teacher.

Location

Because the nature of art making can be very messy, I recommend that you set up the art environment in a space where messes can be welcomed. You may want to "move" your student's art space to areas that make the most sense for each project. For example, I recommend smaller, less messy, more independent, and more manageable art making projects to be done on a table in the Montessori space; and the larger, messier projects should be completed on a table over tile or wood, or in an outside area.

Table

Your table size will not affect your students' abilities to be creative, but the sturdiness of it will. I've witnessed children create beautiful artworks on a surface as large as their lap, so don't feel like your students need a glorious art table.

Chair

Along with a sturdy table, kids need a sturdy chair. Toddlers are movers; they will not always want to sit while making art. Sometimes I introduce activities without chairs so early childhood students can move around the activity and reach art materials easily, but a chair is still good to have at times they're more focused.

No Art Easels

My personal opinion on art easels is very different from most art instructors; I prefer not to teach young kids on easels. I use easels for students over 12 years old. Younger children do not have the fine-motor capabilities needed to control paint drips or work on a slant until they are older. I find it much easier and less frustrating for the child to learn on a flat surface. Easels are fun to pin finished artworks on or for doodling with art supplies that don't run or drip like paint.

Workstations Without Tray Systems

Over the years of observing many Montessori classrooms, I've noticed that teachers stage trays for children to carry their working materials to their activity area. However, I recommend not loading up the trays with art supplies. Art making is different than playing with blocks, laminated nomenclature cards, or math manipulatives. Art materials are generally messy, smear, have pigments that can stain, or spill quickly. Staging shelves is best for students aged 4 or older; materials should be easy to grab and walk with to a workstation. This teaches students the actions of an artist and helps them build those habits.

I also don't recommend children create inside trays, even though it can lessen messes. Working inside a tray limits a child's natural fine-motor capabilities. You want kids to advance and quickly learn how to work as an artist, and trays are cumbersome and not natural to draw, paint, or sculpt inside. Trays are good for keeping supplies and materials grouped together and helping kids understand the tools they need to complete a lesson, but I recommend against children creating inside any type of tray system.

Storage

You can probably attest to the fact that toddlers love to open drawers, cabinets, boxes, anything they can get their hands on—that's why it's important to store art supplies where children can't easily get into. Stash paints, craft supplies, markers, anything small young children can choke on, or anything that needs your watchful eye on in a space that's out of reach. This might mean a high shelf or in a container with a closing mechanism or latch your students can't open.

Art Shelf

Although an art shelf isn't necessary, I highly recommend it as an option for art making inspiration and activities. This space serves as a place where your students can have easy access to the materials they're able to use on their own (those they won't choke on or make a mess with). Place these items in baskets, jars, or trays so they can make projects as they choose. This shelf can also be a springboard for inspiration if you stage it with beautiful books, models, nature elements, toys, and lovely artworks.

Containers for Staging Mediums

Use natural baskets, white colored trays, and clear glass jars for staging art materials. You want kids to be able to distinguish colors and not be distracted by bright color combinations from the containers. You want kids to be able to see the differences between dark green or light green, and a neutral background (i.e. container) will help them do so.

Floor Covering

Wherever you decide to place an art making space, you'll need to consider the chance of regular spills. For this reason, make sure you set up the art space off carpets; tile, wood, patio, or concrete are easier to clean when messes do happen. If you're still concerned about stains, you can purchase a floor covering (like a tarp or cheap rug) for your students to work on.

Carpet Activities

Simple crafts tha t do not utilize glue, paint, or sewing needles can be done on a carpet. For example, doodling with pencils or crayons can be done on carpet because they don't smear. However, I recommend that most of the domains be explored on a flat surface to help the child develop regular artist habits.

Smock

Not every art project will require a smock, since some of them (like drawing, building, and sewing) aren't very messy. Asking your students to wear smocks—and giving them a place to keep it—can help them understand that some art projects can be messy, and help them build great artist habits.

Light Source

A good light source is important for children to create visual art. All art projects are colorful and need a light to identify the varying pigments and color hues. Natural sunlight is the best, but a bright desk lamp can work just as well.

Art Materials To Use & Practical Tips

Choosing the Most Appropriate Art Materials for Early Childhood

The reason why some art supplies and materials are not suitable for this age group is because early childhood students are in what I identify as the "Young Exploratory Phase™." This means they make and create by exploratory and discovery play. Children in these beginning years do not understand the placement of visual arts, but they are very curious about different mediums; they're still working through gross-to-fine motor abilities and are often still putting objects in their mouths. So it's important to choose the right safe mediums and materials as an introduction to visual arts as they experiment and learn from the results they create.

I've met thousands of teachers all over the world who want to start teaching art in their classroom, but they don't know where to start or what materials they need. It's taken me years to amass my own art material collection, so I can understand why trying to purchase the right art material for a classroom all at once can be overwhelming—especially if you have no idea where to start.

When you're teaching art to early childhood Montessori students, you can get by with just a few basic materials. It's just important to be smart and strategic in purchasing those materials. I'd encourage you to start buying a few items to get you started, then adding to it as the year goes on and you start to see your students grow in excitement and interest!

*Note: A shopping list of the bare-basic mediums and materials is provided at the end of this chapter.

Paints

Finger paint
DIY veggie paint
Dry watercolor pod trays
Liquid paint (washable tempera, watercolor, acrylic; use only student-grade non-toxic)
Tempera doodle sticks
Dot paint stampers

Painting Tools

Paintbrushes (different sizes, short handles)
Sponges, sponge stampers
Cups, bowls (for holding paint)
Tubs (for holding water or watercolor paints)
Wash jar
Palette (large and small wells)
Paint rollers
Smock

Objects to Make Fun Textures

Fingers
Potato stamps
Rubber stamps
Bubble wrap
Spray bottle
Alphabet rubber letters
Textured fabrics and string

Painting Tip: Use Only Water-Soluble Paints

All paints for kids should be water-soluble. This means no paint thinner solvents or artist chemicals are needed to work with the paint, only water.

Right- vs. Left-Handed Painting

Depending on which hand your student is more dominant with, I recommend setting up a student's painting station to complement their dominant hand, or hand they use most. When children are very young, it is often difficult to decipher whether they are right- or left-handed. If you are unsure, ask your student which hand they use most when eating or picking up a drinking cup. You can also test this by setting a paintbrush up in front of the child and seeing which hand they reach with. Then set the painting station to help develop the child's gross motor skills by allowing them to reach tools better. You don't want right-handed kids leaning over and dragging their arm across their work to reach their paint palette and wash jar on their left side. You want kids to learn painting skills quickly and learn how to get fine motor control of painting. So set kids up for success and put all their working tools on their right side if they are right-hand dominant and on the left side if they are left-hand dominant. This will lessen spills and help kids to not mess up artworks. This has proven highly successful for me in teaching very young children to paint quickly like an artist.

How Kids Should Hold a Paintbrush

Because children are learning to write and hold a pencil during their early childhood ages, it is the most natural way a child should hold a paintbrush as well. This gives kids the maximum control over their paintbrush. So if you see a child holding a paintbrush awkwardly and having a hard time, show them the natural movements of making a pencil mark with their paintbrush. Tell them to hold it the same way they hold a pencil. Over the years observing children painting and drawing, I've seen some children hold their tools uniquely different than most children. If a child over the age of seven already writes differently than most kids, they will most likely hold a paintbrush in this same manner. I recommend allowing him or her to do what feels most natural and gives them more fine motor control over their paintbrush. It's very difficult to rewire a child's brain pattern of fine motor function, so I do not recommend you insist they paint any differently, as you could stifle their creativity and deter them from wanting to explore painting.

Demonstrate How to Use a Paintbrush

I always demonstrate a brush stroke and how to use all the tools in the paint station. Most likely, early childhood students will not understand the function of a paintbrush. But once you demonstrate how to dip it into the palette and make marks on a surface, they can see with their own eyes how to use a paintbrush and what it's for. It's always best for children to learn by example, so take the time to physically show kids what their tools are used for.

Demonstrate 5 Steps to Painting

1. Dip a paintbrush into the palette;

2. Make a mark on the surface;

3. Wash the paintbrush out in the wash jar;

4. Wipe the wet paintbrush on the napkin; and

5. Dip the paintbrush in another color within the palette and make another brush stroke on the same surface.

By this point, kids are super eager to take over and experiment on their own!

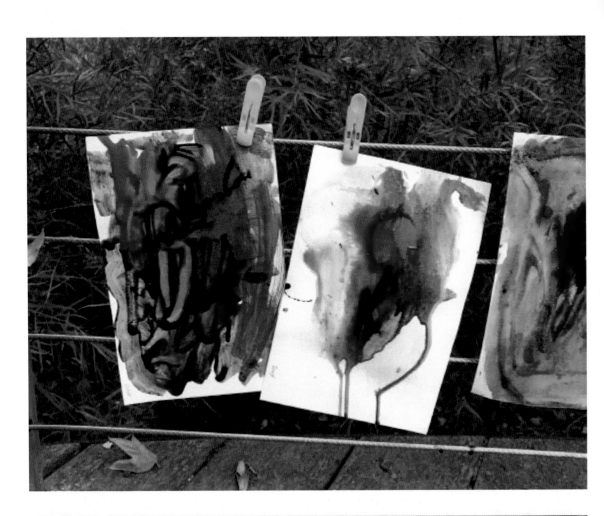

Beware of Dark Pigments Making a Gray Mass

I have spoken to hundreds of teachers who expressed frustration at how most young kids' paintings turn into a gray mass of colors as they create. My explanation is this: Young kids lack the experience and understanding of how dark pigments are strong and can change the tone of light pigments. It's not until kids have lots of experience with dark colors that they understand how to control this.

My solution is to limit too many dark pigments in the young painter's palette until they truly understand how dark pigments overpower light colors. I usually limit dark pigments until five years, when more controlled fine-motor skills take place.

Black does teach important lessons on how to mix different shades in advanced color theory. Black is the darkest pigment besides blue and violet. Lots of mixing with the dark colors of black, dark blue, dark greens, and violet shows kids how strong dark pigments change their lighter pigments with little effort. Controlled mixing like this takes years of practice. There comes a time when kids understand how to control dark pigments in their palette with ease. Until then, use black for brush stroke making independently from other colors.

Use Light Pigments for Toddler Painting

Having fewer dark choices works best when working with early childhood students. Toddlers are just learning how to mix and keep colors inside their palettes. Focus on using more light pigments for younger kids; this type of setup will help them learn fine-motor control and experiment without a dark mess. As they grow and get more refined with using a paintbrush, you can add smaller amounts of paints and more dark-color choices.

Painting Tip: How to Keep Students' Clothes Clean

Painting is a fun yet messy activity that usually gets on clothes. Planning ahead for these types of messes can provide hours of creative fun and give you peace of mind. Always have students wear clothing they can get messy in while doing art. Similar to play clothes, students should have art clothes. It's also helpful if you wear clothes that can get messy because you will get very close to these paints while helping set up. It's been my experience that young toddlers run to their teachers in excitement during painting, so beware and wear art clothes too!

Kids can cover up with a smock or old shirt. Smocks are similar to a cooking apron. Students who've shown up to my painting class with nice clothes found out how paint quickly spreads around. Some of my students at their very first class came with nice clothes and got paint all over them, so now those are their regular painting clothes they return in weekly.

If a student shows up with a very nice shirt, here is a quick tip that works great. Turning their shirts or blouses inside out keeps paint on the side that no one can see when you turn it back. If you're a teacher in a classroom, send friendly reminders home to parents so they can send their kids to school wearing the appropriate clothing for paint day. The idea here is to be sure kids wear clothes appropriate for painting. Maybe even pick a day of the week they can expect painting activities, so they know when to dress kids in artsy type clothes for that day every week.

Painting Tip: Drying Artworks

Over the years of teaching, I've devised ways for my students' paintings to dry without making extra mess or getting ruined, and to help them travel safely home from class. Almost everything kids paint will need time to dry. Outdoor sunlight is the best and quickest way to dry paint projects. Paints in cooler temperatures take more time to dry. If you need to speed up the process of drying, then sunlight or a warm lamp over painted areas can help.

Some paintings will be moist and others will have thick paint and need extra time for drying. Acrylic is one of the faster drying paints and watercolor takes the longest to dry because papers are usually absorbed through.
Laying artworks flat is the best way for them to dry. Projects with more than one side with paint on them need to be propped up somehow. If one side smears, let the opposite side dry completely before the child touches it up so he or she can have a dry side to hold or lay flat on without smearing wet paint again. If you are laying artworks outdoors to dry, you may want to add some weight in case a wind blows. I use rocks found around landscapes as weights.

How to Support Painting

Here are some tips on how you can support creative painting sessions:

Flow & Concentration
Independence
Exploration & Discovery
Creative Experimentation
Freedom Within Limits

Support Flow & Concentration

Allow uninterrupted periods of creative time while your students are working. When you don't interrupt children's painting, they can enter more creative states of flow with heightened concentration. Children can concentrate and go deeper into learning new ideas when not interrupted. To help with these states of flow, try to observe your students from a distance. Too often, creative flow is interrupted by teachers or parents. You should practice more uninterrupted work periods by being conscious of how you are interacting with your child during their painting sessions.

Support Independence

You can support your students' independence by preparing their art environment to support their painting independence. Think about how you have arranged their painting space. Is their working space aligned with their level of abilities? Is their drying area nearby and easy for them to hang or lay their paintings on? Are materials all set up and easy for them to reach so they can get to work? Have you given them the right amount of demonstrations so they know how to use all the materials properly? By revisiting demonstrations, you can support your child to work more independently.

Support Exploration & Discovery

Exploration and discovery can come in many ways. Allow your children the freedom to choose their materials, such as paint colors, and paint brush sizes. You can even give them the freedom to choose the size of papers they want to paint on. Children flourish when they can explore how materials behave or even discover how they work in different ways. The process of exploration and discovery is the best way young children learn painting skills. Allow for lots of discovery time. Young children learn to paint over a long period of time. Try supporting more exploration and discovery rather than the outcome.

Support Creative Experimentation

When children go into different directions than you had planned, take a deep breath and allow their experimentation to happen. Example: If they do not use the paintbrush the way you demonstrated or do not choose the colors you planned in your example. You might be thinking, "Green would look lovely for painting turtles," but your student thinks, "Purple turtles are better!" If your child uses their fingers to paint instead of the paintbrush you took time to stage, as long as they are safe and not disrespecting the art materials, simply allow this type of creative experimentation to go on. This is truly considered one of the artistic processes the National Core Art Standards supports; it's called **INVESTIGATE!**

Support Freedom Within Limits

YES, discovery and exploration are part of the creative process, but we can provide freedom within limits by presentations and demonstrations that support healthy limits. We can demonstrate where painting will take place, where it's accepted in the art environment, and where it's NOT allowed. One of the biggest lessons I learned early on, is that you need to explain to children where painting is not allowed, like the walls, and how walking around with loaded paint brushes is not allowed outside of their art workspace. I also explain to children how to set up and clean up when they are done painting. As a homeschool mom, I even had to explain this to my own children while they weregrowing up. The freedom should be in what they want to express or paint but not where they want to paint.

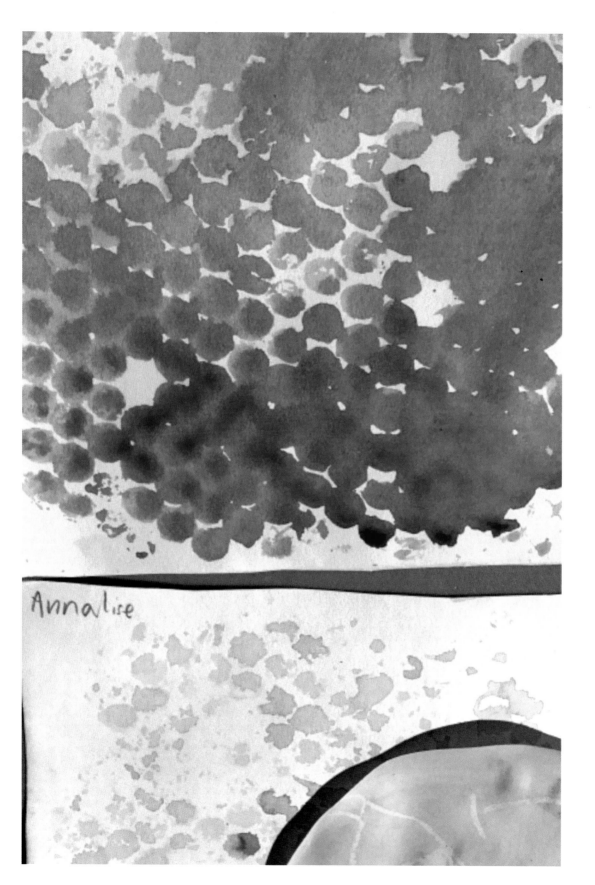

Annalise

Painting Tip: What Kids Can Paint On

Traditional painting lessons are taught on stretch canvases but this can get costly when early childhood students are just beginning to learn the medium. I've come up with time-tested, low-cost surfaces on which to teach painting skills. Plenty of painting practice and color mixing experiences can be achieved by altering paint surfaces. Also, painting different surfaces from time to time will create high interest and less boredom. All kids are at different levels of fine-motor capabilities, so having different surfaces to paint rather than always relying on their own imagination to conjure up images on a blank canvas or paper is a good option. Kids can actually refine painting skills by simply painting lots of different surfaces and objects!

Alternate paint surfaces:

Watercolor paper
Handcrafted paper
Rocks
Sticks & branches
Tiny to large pieces of woodcrafts, small blocks of wood
Butcher block paper
Cardboard boxes
Canvas
Muslin fabric rolls
Toilet paper rolls
Recycled woodcrafts
Plastic sun catchers
Air-dried magic clay forms
Egg cartons
Old CDs
Large seed pods
Pine cones
T-shirts
Shower curtain
Large collaborative banners
Garden signs
Seashells
Maps
Newsprint
Cans and canisters
Old recycled books
Pumpkins
Gourds

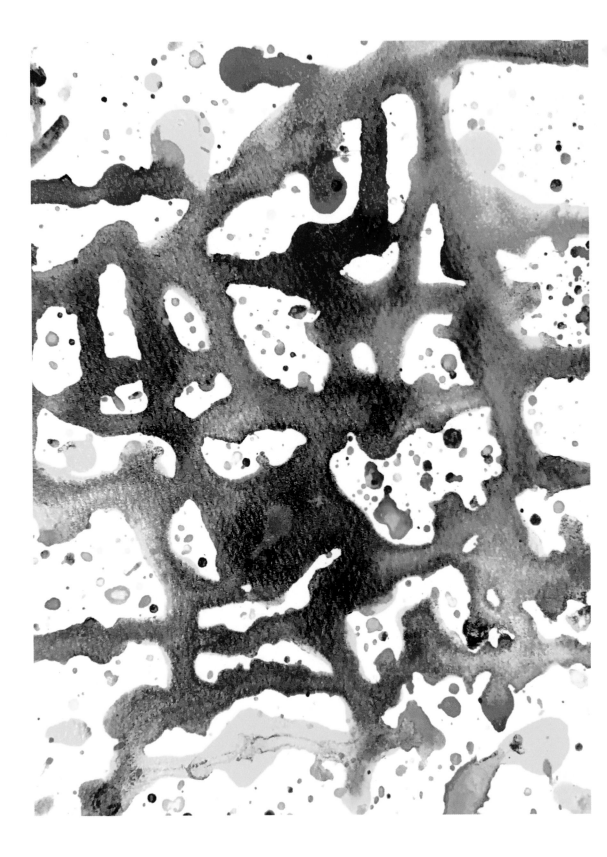

Color Theory

Basic Color Theory Materials:

Primary colors (red, yellow and blue)
Glass Droppers (3-6)
Plastic squeeze bottles
Color wheel chart
Paint Brushes
Mixing palette
Wash jar
Watercolor paper

Color Theory Lesson Activity: Watercolor Play

Here's what you need to know about setting up Watercolor Play. I recommend setting up this art lesson on a regular basis—maybe once a month, or even once a week—so early childhood students' understanding consistently grows and deepens. You'll see that it's super easy to put together too, so you don't have to stress or think too much about the activity.

Materials

Watercolor paint is the foundation of this activity, but everything else— buckets, tubs, bowls, brushes, etc.—are what lead to new discoveries.

Here's what you need for Watercolor Play: kid-safe, non-toxic liquid paint (acrylic, tempera, or watercolor) that's been watered down to be transparent (try one part paint to five parts water)

Bottles with adjustable caps OR clear plastic tubs

Bowls, cups

Paintbrushes, sponges, stampers, drippers

Watercolor paper or other thick (optional)

Aprons or old clothes

How To Watercolor Play

What I love about this activity, is that it's so simple to set up! Plus, you can mix things up every time you put it together to give your students new experiences and keep expanding their curiosity.

NOTE: This project should be set up outdoors or somewhere where you're comfortable with water being splashed (i.e., tile, not rugs or carpet). This project can get messy with younger children, since most toddlers don't yet have the fine motor skills or dexterity to control what they're doing. But a little mess is all part of the fun! And you don't have to worry about permanent stains, since most kids' paint is washable.

There are really only three steps for Watercolor Play:
1. Put all your materials out on a table
2. Let kids explore and play
3. Place artworks in the drying area

The best part of all this, is that kids do all the discovery play work on their own; you don't have to lead any lesson or make things technical. Just let them play with the colors and mix things naturally, they'll create their own colors and see things for themselves. If they're old enough to ask about colors, then you can go ahead and start naming the general hues, and hint at what adding other colors might do to change the original color (i.e. make it lighter).

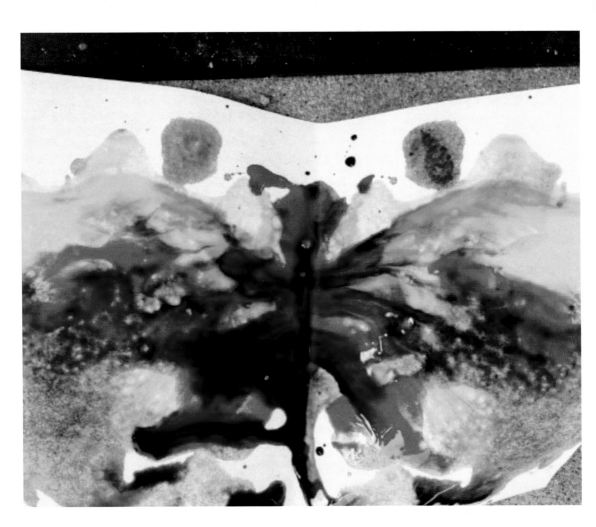

Doodling & Drawing

Doodling & Drawing Mediums

Crayons (in different sizes and shapes)
Colored pencils (jumbo and short sized are easier for toddlers to grip)
Crayon rubbings
Graphite pencils (jumbo sized are easier for toddlers to grip)
Tri-colored-tip color pencils
Doodling & Drawing Tools
Crayon rubbings
Paper
Pencil sharpener

Doodling & Drawing Tip: Working with Smaller Paper

Cut full-size papers into smaller pieces and place them into simple baskets. If
you come to one of my art classes you will find several baskets of small-cut,
high-quality papers. Kids are not yet capable of planning out projects, so I don't
feel early childhood kids should use large quality pieces of paper for exploring.
Working with smaller cuts stops kids from scribbling on large pieces of paper
andthrowing them away before grabbing another one. Young kids also have small
hands and don't have the capabilities to work long periods to cover a large paper
or fill it up with ideas. I have seenchildren draw right in the center of a large
paper and then grab another for another artwork idea.

If you take standard 8 1/2" x 11" piece of paper, you could trim out four drawing papers and give students four opportunities to create different ideas. I'm not opposed to giving kids larger pieces of paper, but this method gives kids a chance to practice first. I have never had a student from my classes or workshops complain about the smaller paper size. I do offer larger pieces of paper to a child that has a plan and knows what they want to draw or paint out.

Another reason for this is environmental commitment. Teaching these values can help students make connections to their planet and help them understand their consumer habits. You can provide high quality type papers kids can use at a fraction of the normal cost and save trees.

Typical paper sizes I have are 8 1/2 x 11 cut to quarters; half of 8 1/2 x 11 is 5 1/2 x 8 1/2; then half of 5 1/2 x 8 1/2 trims down to 4.25 x 5 1/2 piece of paper. I do this with watercolor, pastel, drawing, and tracing paper.

Toddler

Working with smaller papers may not work with 13 months - 3 years because they are working on gross motor skills. I recommend large group papers using butcher-block paper covered on surfaces while young kids learn to hold and use doodling supplies. Most kids get fine motor control between three years to five years. Before that it's very gross and shared surfaces to doodle work great. I always have a coloring table covered with butcher-block paper for free doodling at these ages. I change the paper out when it gets covered up with doodles. Staging a doodling station can be as simple as laying paper down and providing a basket full of crayons.

How-to prepare an Art Doodle Coloring Station for Toddlers

I host creative events and art classes for children regularly. Teachers love how I set up fun art spaces, and want to know how can they mimic this in their spaces. So here's my quick tips for setting up this inviting doodling stations for little ones. Believe it or not, it's very simple to set up and you too can create this welcoming coloring station that will excite students. You can prepare this space in a tiny area, classroom, or even outdoors.

What you'll need:
Low table for toddlers to reach
Chairs (optional), kids usually don't mind standing or kneeling.
You will need to keep an eye on young tots with small chairs.
Large roll of paper, craft or butcher block paper found in craft stores or online.

Doodling supplies:
crayons, colored pencils, and pencils.
A well-lit area so kids can see colors.
Magnifying glass
Ruler
Paper cutter (for teacher use only)

Preparing table:
Step 1. Cut paper to table size with scissors.
Step 2. Fasten to table with tape (large tape, such as clear or masking tape, works best).
Step 3. Place doodling supplies out to invite kids to create.
Step 4. Make some inviting marks so small children understand it's okay to draw on the large paper.

White- or natural-colored paper with dark pigmented drawing materials is easier for little retinas to detect. If you are doing projects with dark colored paper be sure to use pigments that are contrasting and bright so line edges are easier to detect

123

Clay Modeling

Clays Types

Homemade playdough (made with flour, salt, cream of tartar, water, vegetable or coconut oil, essential oils, and food coloring)
Non-hardening plasticine clay
Earth pottery air-dry clay

Clay Tools

Carving and cutting tools
Cookie cutters of any shape Spatula
Stamps
(Ages 3-6) Solid geometric forms
(Ages 3-6) Tile for working on top

Gather fun decorating elements:
Glass beads
Beans
Seeds
Herbs
Twigs
Pebbles

Clay Modeling Tip: Toddler Caution!

Are you worried about young children putting small embellishments into their mouths? Keep it simple with clay, rolling pins, cookie cutters, and large twigs. Progress later when the child is past the stage of putting items into their mouth.

Teach Simple Movements First

Start by introducing early childhood students to simple movements when they first start working with clay.

These include:

Pinching
Squishing
Patting
Rolling balls
Back and forth motion (with a rolling pin)
Pressing
Poking
Tearing
Cutting and slicing (with a wood-modeling tool)
Carving
Digging
Clay Modeling Tip: Teach Simple Forms Second
Once students master simple movements, move on to creating simple forms:
Ropelike coils / snakes
Slabs
Rounded and circular shapes
Mountain peaks
Cubes
Cylinder pyramids / triangles
Teardrops
Flat pancakes
Cookie-cutter shapes
Older kids

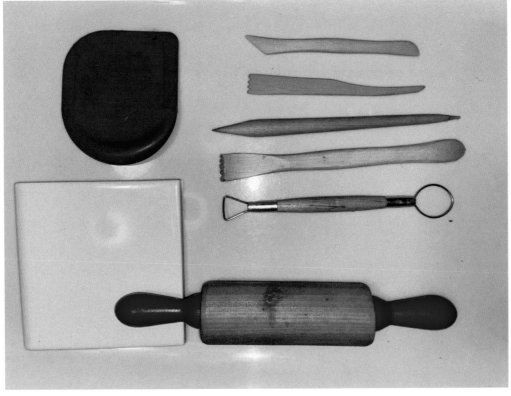

Clay Modeling: Teach Simple Forms Second

Once students master simple movements, move on to creating simple forms:

- Ropelike coils / snakes
- Slabs
- Rounded and circular shapes
- Mountain peaks
- Cubes
- Cylinder pyramids / triangles
- Teardrops
- Flat pancakes
- Cookie-cutter shapes

Older kids can learn to attach clay parts with carving tools, wire, tooth picks, and learn score and slip methods.

Clay Modeling Lesson Activity:

Beginner Model-Building Projects, Cookie Cutter Forms

Making shapes from cookie cutters is easy for early childhood students. All you need is a variety of cookie cutter shapes. Shapes can be embellished with all the lovely items listed in this book. Start off with a wedge of clay as big as the child's fist. You also want to consider the cookie cutter size, be sure there's enough for cut out.

How-to:

1. Make a round ball by rolling on a table surface or between hands.
2. Flatten ball into pancake shape, then roll flat with a rolling pin, until it is about ¼ inch thick.
3. Press cookie cutter into clay, clear away extra clay around outside edges of cookie cutter shape and push cut shape out gently. This takes lots of practice.
4. Have children decorate by pressing and pushing embellishments into clay.
5. Use spatula to slide under forms to move to drying area. Using a spatula helps keep form together when moving them around. Pottery clay is very sticky and will usually stick to the surface the child is working on, so a spatula helps move and unstick to surfaces.

*Note: The more a child presses and rolls out a clay slab, the thinner and wider it'll become. Too thin of a slab will be hard to pick up with a spatula, which can ruin their creation. Try to help kids keep slabs no thinner than a quarter of an inch. This takes practice and is part of exploring clay properties. You can roll out slabs and make cut out shapes for younger kids who have not developed their fine-motor skills. After a while kids will enjoy doing the whole process independently.

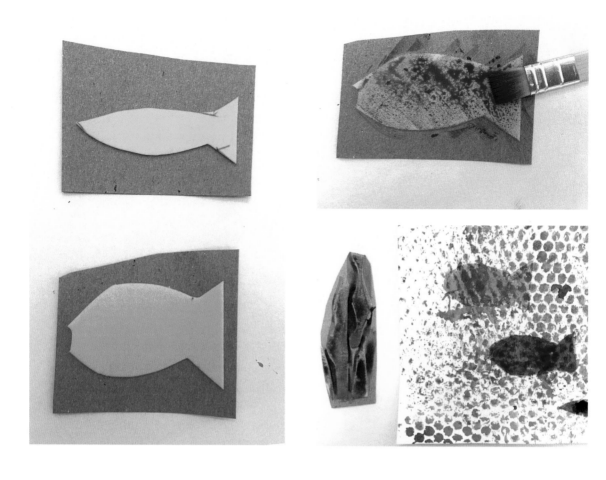

Crafting & Building

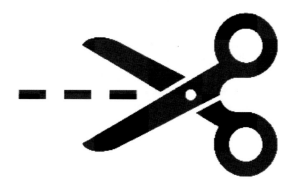

How to Teach Important Scissor Skills to Early Childhood Students

If I told you that I often lead students in Montessori early childhood scissor cutting, I'm sure you—and many other teachers—might be a little concerned (to say the least). Giving scissors to a young child might seem crazy, or dangerous, at the very least. But it's an essential skill everyone needs, and if it's taught correctly, early childhood students can master it too.

You see, using scissors is a great way for young students to develop their fine motor skills. So while it can be a little scary to hand a pair of (blunt-tip) scissors to a three-year-old, it'll eventually help them perform many other activities around the classroom.

In fact, the earlier a child can learn to use scissors, the better. The activity provides so many benefits to early childhood students! Being able to properly use scissors opens the doors to many other important skills, such as writing their names or ABCs, tying shoes, zipping jackets, cleaning up, and feeding themselves.

So, how do you know when your early childhood students are actually ready to start using scissors?

If your students can sit and focus on an activity for at least 15 minutes, they should be able to learn and start practicing their scissor cutting. You'll need your students to be able to sit through a complete Montessori early childhood scissor cutting demonstration, where you present the basic movements and show how to safely handle the tool. So, if they can keep their attention on your presentation and understand the necessary outcome, then they can start practicing. Just make sure you're supervising early childhood students any time they are using scissors.

Importance of Scissor Cutting to Early Childhood Development

By showing young students—even as young as two or three years—how to use scissors, you're helping them reach critical milestones that directly related to other areas of childhood development. The dynamic motion that comes from cutting activities—specifically, opening and closing scissors along a distinct path—helps them build muscle control, develop eye and hand coordination, deepen their tactile spatial awareness, and hone their fine-motor movements. It also helps them develop the coordination needed for handwriting, eating, dressing, and holding and carrying small objects.

A child that has scissor practice will be able to excel in complex steps to create and work independently. And they'll be able to do so many artful and creative things in the classroom, such as cutting paper, following patterns, cutting strings and yarn, and cutting fabric.

Where to Start: Montessori Early Childhood Scissor Cutting Lessons

You can't hand your early childhood students a pair of scissors and then walk away expecting them to create, it's an early childhood art material that needs to be taught how to use. It's important to give them time to practice the simple movements of just using scissors. Once they have that down, then you can start introducing students to cutting for copy-mode or process-based activities.

Materials:
Safety scissors (with a blunt tip)
Soft, thick yarn
Styrofoam sheets
Construction paper
Clay

5 Early Childhood Scissor Cutting Lesson Ideas:

1. Have children cut small and large lengths of yarn.
2. Students can cut large shapes from styrofoam, and then glue them onto paper.
3. Show students how to roll out coils of clay, and then cut those into small pieces
4. Give students pieces of construction paper that have lines or shapes drawn onto them (or ask the kids to draw their own lines and shapes), and have them cut along the lines.
5. Try incorporating some of these lesson ideas with other topics you're already teaching in the classroom. For example, make some of the shapes organic, like leaves or simple animal silhouettes.

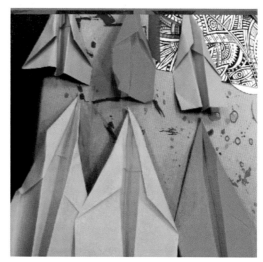

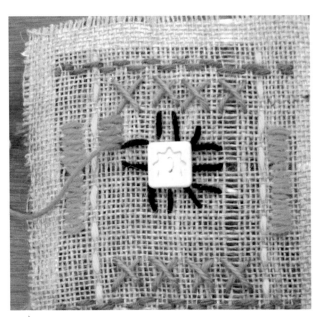

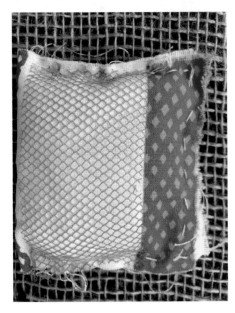

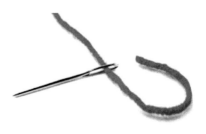

Crafting Tools

Safety scissors
Glue
Tape
*Sewing needle
Weaving loom
*Glue gun (set at a low temperature, with supervision)
*Starch (craft starch for paper products, like paper mache)
*Stapler
*Note: The starred materials and tools are not suitable for toddlers; they should be saved for children in later early childhood, ages 3-6.

Crafting Materials

Almost anything here can be collected and used to build, construct, and craft. You can pick some of these items up from any school or craft supply store, but most of these can be collected or recycled items from around your home, school, or classroom.

Beads (with supervision for toddlers)
Pom poms (with supervision for toddlers)
Foam sheets
Nature elements
Paper
Recycled materials
String
Wood and popsicle sticks
Magazines
Construction paper, thick multi-colors
Egg cartons
Paper mask
Paper rolls
Cardboard containers, from tiny to large
Shoe boxes, or any small box
Packing envelopes (save shipping envelopes like Fedex or other thick envelopes)
Folders (filing folders of any color)
Paper plates
Coffee filters
Milk cartons
*Toothpicks
Balloons (with supervision for all ages)
*Straws
Feathers, a variety of color options
Fabric, of any kind
Yarn, a variety of color options
Felt, a variety of color options
Wool, a variety of color options
Pipe Cleaners, a variety of colors
Embellishments, buttons, glitter, or googly eyes (with supervision for toddlers)

Craft Activity Ideas

What can you build or construct with all these items? Many of these activities are recommended for early childhood students ages 4-6 years old.

Natural Art Arrangements: Mandalas

Weavings

Collages

Music makers

Bird feeders

Masks

Robots

Vegetable and plant 3-D models

Miniature vegetable garden

Cardboard dioramas of animals, sea life, and insects

Wind chimes

Garden planters

Miniature cities and buildings

Cardboard weaving

Miniature cars, trains, planes, rockets, or boats

Miniature barns

Cardboard games

Maps

Cell models

Solar system models

Botany models

Life cycle models (for animals, sea animals, and insects)

Layers of the Earth models

Landform models and dioramas

3-D charts and maps

Ecosystem dioramas

Art Collaging

Collaging gives students the ability to express their creativity and even helps them develop their fine-motor skills. That's why art collaging activities are great to introduce. The activity involves the process of selecting, assembling, and pasting a variety of materials down into a unique arrangement. It's an ideal craft for early childhood students because collages are intuitive arrangements; they're the perfect artful playground for kids to craft in. First plane students, 3-6 years, are ready for simple collage making crafts. This is an exciting age for art making, since they're likely crafting and exploring different art mediums for the very first time!

Early childhood students are able to hold materials, practice scissor cutting, and explore the different collaging mediums tactilely. They can dip a paintbrush into glue, learn to paste, and make simple arrangements. It's best to keep instructions simple—giving them just one- or two-step instructions. (For example, cut and paste; or paste and arrange.)

It's best for early childhood students to work in process-based mode (or creative-mode), which means art making focuses on the process, not the outcome. Again, any copy-mode creating should be basic; with simple instructions meant to build implicit memory. You should allow students to try Montessori early childhood art collaging without any expected outcome.

Where to Start: Simple Collaging Activities

Children at 3-6 years are very curious about materials and how they can be used. At this age, they're very quick learners! By introducing art collaging you can actually help refine their small motor muscles, since the activity involves making controlled movements through cutting, pasting, and manipulating the collaging mediums.

Keep collage materials very basic at first. I'd suggest starting with light-weight paper and glue sticks. This gives students the opportunity to learn more about how adhesive works, and they'll be able to build upon that skill as they create more and more. After they've had a few chances to explore this type of art activity, you'll see that they'll likely have a decent understanding of how collaging works, and will want to create with new types of materials. Collaging can be done with any type of material: paper, fabric, natural elements, recycled objects (buttons, tiny beads, pieces of cardboard, etc.), sequins, foil, glass, wire, and burlap. However, since young children are still developing their fine-motor skills, make sure the objects are easy to grasp, pinch, or hold.

They can also be a little impatient at this age, so you also want to make sure the objects they're crafting with can be easily pasted onto their working surface. (You don't want things falling off their canvas, and you don't want to have to use a glue gun to make sure their designs stay in place!) Tape can also be used in place of adhesive glues and pastes; washi tape comes in a bunch of fun designs and can add to the art they're creating! Be sure to give children plenty of time to experiment with making different arrangements. It takes some time to understand how to paste, arrange, and press down or hold their design objects into place to create the look they desire.

Planning Activities & Presentations

Weekly Themed Activities

I recommend alternating art "themes." For instance, start with painting one week; let your students play with watercolor paints one day, then dry painted artwork, then on the following day you can introduce sponges or dot stampers. Then the next week, allow them to explore drawing, and give them new drawing art materials to play with each day.

Early childhood students need a lot of time to process and play with each different art material in order to really understand how they work and what they can create. I recommend sticking to one theme each week; it gives young children the time they need to learn an idea. Plus, it will cut back on any chance that your students will become overstimulated or overwhelmed. Only working within one area a week also makes things easier on you!

If you're focusing on clay this week, you can keep painting, drawing, building, and crafting supplies put away and out of sight until they're needed. That means only setting up the clay supplies once, at the beginning of the week, instead of bringing out new materials every single day.

Once you've allowed your students to explore each area of visual art (drawing, painting, clay sculpting, crafting, and building), you can make the next round of discovery fresh and exciting by using story books as inspiration and changing the inspiration. Use the book The Very Hungry Caterpillar for example: read them the book, let them soak up the beautiful artwork, and then encourage them to create their own caterpillar out of clay. Or, explore painting, ask them to paint a big green leaf, using different shades and colors of green, for the Hungry Caterpillar to eat.

Teaching can be so much fun! As a teacher, it's exciting to see them light up as they explore different mediums and grow in their confidence and creativity. As a child, it's a chance to jump into a whole new world of color and experiences.

Theme Examples

Week 1: Painting
Monday - Finger painting, focus on one color
Tuesday - Sponge painting, focus on one color and texture
Wednesday - Tempera paint stick dooding, focus on lines
Thursday - Potato stamp painting, focus on color and shape
Friday - Brushstroke painting, focus color and curved lines

How to Teach Art Lessons Without Compromising Creativity

Art and creativity usually go hand in hand, but I've seen so many teachers overteach their students when it comes to art—giving them step-by-step instructions and expecting every student's final art project to look the same—but this stifles creativity! If you've been teaching like this, I'm willing to bet it's because that's how you were taught (especially if you only have limited art experience). But there's a better way! And once you learn how to teach art lessons this way, not only will teaching lessons become easier for you, but you'll also be promoting creativity in your students.

Because creativity is actually a pretty great concern amongst Montessori teachers. In fact, I'm often asked how to teach art lessons without compromising student creativity. I like to answer this question by first explaining what it means to be creative. And once you understand what creativity is, you'll understand how to encourage it—not compromise it.

What is creativity?

Being creative means coming up with a completely new idea—something novel, something never designed before, or something conjured up from one's own imagination. For children to think this way, we have to get out of their way and not disturb their creative process. We have to relinquish control of the end product. Thankfully, as teachers, we're used to giving our students the space to work independently; now, it's just about learning how to teach art lessons that support their independence and creativity.

Balancing Teaching Art Lessons and Allowing for Creativity

While it's okay to show step-by-step instructions and use inspirational examples, you don't want to insist on what students' end-project should look like. It can be tempting to fall into detailed instructions and lessons, but that doesn't give students the freedom to be creative.

As you plan your Montessori art lessons, ask yourself these questions:

Are you asking your students to copy step-by step instructions?

Do you have an art sample of what the outcome should look like?

Is your art lesson rigid, with no flexibility for kids to invent or create a new idea?

Do you discourage your students from exploring and experimenting with mediums (i.e. they must use it the "correct" way)?

If you answered yes to these questions, you are teaching copy-mode lessons and likely with step-by-step instructions—and are definitely going to compromise creativity. To support more creativity in your classroom, you have to adjust your lessons. Allow more freedom to explore, experiment and finish the art project in any direction.

You can support creativity by teaching through process-based or choice-based methods. Choice-based teaching provides students the freedom to choose their art project, mediums, and make anything they choose. Process-based teaching is all about exploration and discovery—not the end result or what that final product is going to look like. Both of these methods allow kids to flow into their own creations without adhering to rules of what to create; they instill the idea that there is no right or wrong way to create and make art.

Where to Start: Montessori Art Lesson Creativity Guides

It's possible to teach high-quality art skills without compromising creativity. The idea is to give your students a prompt to start with or skill set to practice, then let them create.

Here are five ways to start teaching your students creative are lessons:

1. Choose the art project
2. Choose the artistic technique, method, or style to study
3. Demonstrate how to use different mediums
4.. Prepare an art space for exploration and experimentation
5. Allow for flexibility and freedom for kids to create their own ideas

Once you get the hang of it and practice being more hands-off, you'll notice your students coming up with amazing new creative ideas. You will also be better supporting the artistic process and ensuring that students develop art literacy and meet art standards.

Direct and Indirect Aims

Here's how to create effective Montessori art direct and indirect aims. I'm sure you know how important it is to support students in their own self discovery using their hands and senses within the classroom environment. This exploration process is similar to how artists discover and create with their own hands too. Our hands are the neural connection that feeds our brain information; they're also the way we develop and hone our fine-motor skills.

How can you support students in the artistic process and inspire them to think creatively? Start with understanding how direct and indirect aims relate to artistic development and progression.

For an artist to create, they must move through the artistic process, which is the four actions an artist experiences while creating and producing artworks. It starts with self discovery through their hands, then designing with their imaginations, then constructing with materials, and finally, reflecting about their process through expression by using art language, creative writing, or community sharing.

So let's compare these actions to Montessori's method of direct and indirect aims to teaching as a guide.

Art Lesson: Direct Aims

In an artistic environment, your Montessori art direct aim can be to prepare the work space, explore different artist materials, and manage time for art creation—while following art standards. You can also demonstrate and isolate techniques that promote independent exploration, engagement, and how to work in a respectful, artful way within the classroom.

The Artistic Process: Indirect Aims

Indirect aims are accomplished by stepping back and allowing the artistic process's four actions to unfold. Self discovery by sensory tactile spatial exploration with the eyes, hands and mind; improvisation and creative selection of the elements and principles of design; the hands-on construction of ideas; and finally, the opportunity to reflect on the process verbally or through writing. Indirect aims unfold during the artistic process. Creativity is the result of the process.

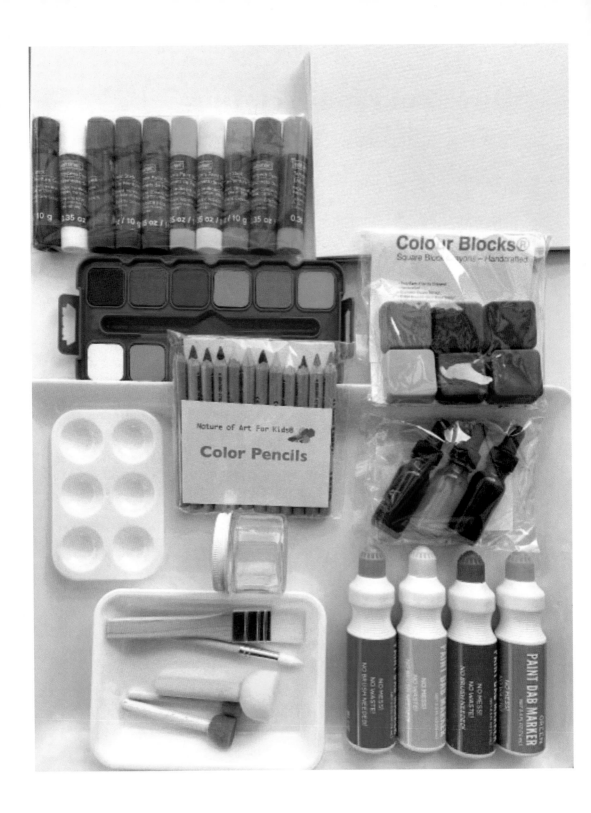

Safety Non-Toxic Guide

Precautionary Principle!

When selecting art supplies for children, I always use the **Precautionary Principle**. Simply said, "Better to be safe than sorry." Following this simple guide ensures developing young children are safely guarded from any harmful chemicals. Unfortunately, most commercial art supplies do not come with guaranteed conclusive scientific proof that there are no hazardous substances hidden inside them. Even though art supplies are approved in the U.S. and other countries and conform to labeling policy laws, I still use these safety guides as a standard for young kids.

My Safety Standards: I recommend kids under the age of 12 do not use adult-grade paints. Young children do not have a strong immune system compared to adults; our body's immune system helps us resist invading microorganisms. Some chemicals may be safe to use and are not highly toxic, but can cause long-term chronic toxicity to someone with a weak immune system. Effects from chronic toxicity may not appear immediately after the first exposure or even several uses, but may take years to produce symptoms.

Many adult artist-grade art mediums may contain hazardous pigments like cadmium, lead, formaldehyde, or solvents, and they may include special instructions for handling.
Some paints may have additives, mildew resistance substances, or other chemicals. These added chemicals could be harmful to children who are not aware of special handling instrutions.

Always look to see if there is a "**Conforms to ASTM D-4236**" label somewhere on the bottle. "Conforms to ASTM D-4236" means the art supplies are not hazardous and are safe for kids to handle. If you have art supply containers that appear old and you cannot identify the "Conforms to ASTM D-4236," I recommend you do not allow kids to use them. Older art mediums before the "Conforms to ASTM D-4236" law may contain toxic vapors and chemicals.

*Caution : Trying to identify if an art supply is safe by looking for a strong scent does not guarantee there are no harmful chemicals; many toxic chemicals and solvents are odorless.

If you are outside of the U.S. I recommend following the European labeling law with the letters 'CE'.

About the author

Spramani Elaun is author of several art education books. She is a homeschooling mom, art teacher with a natural teaching method and the founder of Nature of Art For Kids® art school & art supply company. After spending thousands of hours teaching young children her visual art method, she now supports teachers and parents on how to use her time-tested art method. Spramani teaches art classes, trains teachers, hosts art workshops at education conferences, guest speaks, and hosts art events internationally. Spramani's educational background; MFA, certification in conceptual arts, graphic design, painting, multimedia, offset printing, digital marking, business marketing management, manufacturing & product design. Spramani's art method is changing the way young children learn visual arts today.

Authors Page

Spramani Elaun
Nature of Art®
P.O. Box 443 Solana Beach,
CA 92075
U.S. 1 + (760) 652-5194

http://montessori-art.com/
http://www.ecokidsart.com/

Email Info@Spramani.com
Whats App +1 (760) 652-5194
WeChat ID Spramani-ArtTeacher

Facebook https://www.facebook.com/montessoriarttribe
Instragram https://www.instagram.com/nature.of.art.for.kids/
Linkedin https://www.linkedin.com/in/ecokidsart/

Author Services:

• Art Events, Workshops & Venue Sponsorship
• Art Classes
• Teacher Art Training
• Personal Development Workshops
• Educational Speaker/Seminars/Keynote
• Art Webinar School Training
• Kids Art Supply Sales
• Corporate Creative Events

Books
Nurturing Children in The Visual Arts Naturally ISBN-13: 978-0991626403
Clay Play ISBN-13: 978-0991626441
Kids Painting Book ISBN-13: 978-0991626410
Kids Color Theory Book ISBN-13: 978-0991626434
Defining Visual Arts 978-0-9916264-5-8
Introducing Visual Arts to the Montessori Classroom ISBN-13: 978-0991626427

Curriculums
Paint Curriculum, 57 brushstroke Lessons
Kids Color Theory Curriculum, 37 mixing Lessons
Clay Modeling, 27 Lessons
Kids Drawing Curriculum

"Just as seeds grow in the natural world with all the right elements, a child's love for art will grow organically if nurtured."

Spramani E'Laun

Made in the USA
Columbia, SC
02 September 2022

66595013R00093